OBSERVATIONS

by

Tom Martin

To: Andne and MAriA
MAy your liver be long, And
filled with much joy And
hoppiness. Merry Christmas.
TM

OBSERVATIONS

First Printing

Copyright © 1998

ISBN 0-930871-04-9

Library of Congress Catalog Card Number: 98-90326

Published by: SEARCH, 106 Sterling Ave., Mt. Sterling, KY 40353

Cover photo: The misty and haunting gaze of Ashes Swango.

FOREWORD

Aesop, in one of his Fables, told of some blind men who were taken to "observe" an elephant. One grabbed its tail and determined that the beast was like a rope. Another felt of a leg and concluded that it must be like a tree. Another laid hands on its trunk and proclaimed that the elephant was much like a snake. All the men were right, to some degree, yet all were very wrong.

Aren't we just like these blind men? We think we know the truth when in fact "we see thru a glass darkly," as the Apostle Paul wrote in the Bible. We observe the world around us and come to conclusions which are sometimes very incorrect. With these erroneous ideas firmly in our mind, we begin to see ourselves as better or different from other people, and we begin building walls, dividing into groups, or setting ourselves apart. Often, when we believe incorrectly about one thing, it will cause us to believe incorrectly about something else, in a very predictable way. Sometimes the lies we believe are so great that it becomes impossible for

continued on page 153

Many people are intimidated
by the credentials of others, but this is
wrong and should not be. Only God
knows who is greatest, and He judges
by things we cannot see.

2

Lack of love isn't caused by racism;
racism is caused by lack of love.

If people were paid according to their value to society, many paupers would become wealthy and many wealthy would become paupers, and farmers might become the best paid people of all.

No matter how educated we are, or how much we know, or how great that we may be, none of us is really willing to know the truth in all things. It is this flaw in human character which most causes the problems between us. It is this flaw which most retards the progress of man.

4

When you can no longer get pleasure out of watching an ant scurry across a sidewalk, you can conclude that you've gotten old.

As long as there is God there is hope, and there is always God.

We often assume that happiness can be increased by owning several of something, instead of just one. More often than not, the more we have of any given thing, the less joy those things will bring us.

People who oppose tight restrictions on pornography almost always support tight restrictions on firearms.

Things which are bad for kids are almost always bad for adults. Most adults never seem to realize this.

People who oppose the use of tobacco rarely rail about the use of alcohol. People who rail about the use of alcohol are usually silent about the use of tobacco.

In a court of law, having a room full of eyewitnesses does not always guarantee the truth. We cannot always believe what we see ourselves, therefore we should not be too quick to believe what others claim to have seen.

Toilet paper is one of the
most important inventions of all time.

10

The best money spent on health care
is the money we spend learning how to
care for our health.

Loud rock concerts usually draw big crowds. Loud church services usually draw big crowds. God usually speaks softly.

The primary purpose of a mountain is so that we might have something to climb.

In the hands of a maniac,
a jug of gasoline can be more deadly
than a gun. Danger comes not from
a weapon, but mainly from the
one who wields it.

12

Many people take great pride in the lands from whence their ancestors came, but for whatever reason, few show any desire to move back there.

A major hallmark of intelligence is an open mind.

It's almost impossible to acquire great wealth if all investment decisions are left to bankers and brokers. It's almost impossible to have optimum health if all medical decisions are left to doctors and hospitals. Success, in most any endeavor, comes from the diligence to acquire knowledge and the courage to make decisions for yourself.

14

Most people would be very
frustrated if the results of their labors
usually got tossed in the trash.
Mail carriers deserve a lot more honor
than we give them.

People who have terminal illnesses
– who have given up all hope –
are the ones most reluctant to try
alternative healing methods.
A wise physician once observed
that "in most diseases,
the brain dies first."

16

Some people see a face as ugly;
other people see the same face as lovely.
These differences of opinion help
assure the survival of our species!

Nice guys often finish last,
but they rarely get venereal disease!

With all the science we have, we cannot truly prove our own existence, much less God's. In reality, we must take everything on faith. Instead of trying to force our beliefs on others, we just need to love each other more. God doesn't need us harassing people to make His existence known.

18

Governments are a reflection of those they govern. More often than not, we get the kind of government we deserve.

Being in a forest evokes a feeling of peace in most people. Maybe we should do more to protect our forests, so that we'll always have a peaceful place to go.

Some people see themselves as old at thirty. Other people see themselves as young at sixty. What age we truly are is greatly determined by what age we perceive ourselves to be.

20

Intelligence is often confused
with knowledge. If knowledge was
intelligence, highly educated people
would seldom do stupid things.

Most people who make big bucks
in the stock market read the Investor's
Business Daily.

M_{any} of us have deformed toes because of wearing tight, pointed-toe shoes. If God had wanted us to wear pointed shoes, we'd all have been born with pointed feet.

22

The more extreme the weather,
the more adventure there is to be found.

The greatest thinking
is often done in the bathroom.

In general, the more money a preacher pays for his car, the less spiritual he will be.

24

⚜

The device which most threatens the survival of man is not the Bomb, but the bulldozer.

All humans have a common fault:
When all is said and done, we believe or
disbelieve, not because of evidence, but
because something deep within us
"wishes" to believe that way. It is exactly
as Jesus pointed out in the parable of
Lazarus and the rich man:
"if someone returned from the grave, they
still would not believe."

If we would think often about the driving mistakes we have made, we might get less angry when other drivers make the same mistakes.

26

People are like trains;
they follow the track.

Many of us are fond of believing
that the things we own are the "very
best." More often than not, our
beliefs are very wrong.

It's a safe bet that people who call you on the phone to sell you something are more interested in fattening their bank account than in fattening your bank account.

People who were executed for committing heinous crimes have never been known to commit the same crimes again.

29

It often seems that the more money a couple spends on their wedding, the shorter their marriage will be.

The healthiest people dine almost exclusively on raw fruits, vegetables, nuts, and seeds. Perhaps the rest of us should eat that way too.

Woolly worms prefer climbing upward. For some reason, they usually hate going down.

Parents sometimes worry too much if their kids aren't making top grades in school. Many great scientists and super-achievers didn't make good grades. When all is said and done, "cream rises." Parents should be concerned more about their children's morals, and less about the grades that they make.

Far more people are harmed each year by cars than are harmed by guns. If we really cared about human life, we'd worry more about who drives cars than about who owns guns.

32

Many of us believe that government is a friend of the people. Others believe that government (although necessary) is an enemy of the people. When reading the things our Founding Fathers wrote, one has to conclude that they saw government as an enemy too.

33

People who believe in rights for unborn children rarely believe in rights for animals. People who believe in rights for animals rarely believe in rights for unborn children.

The best chocolate is not
always the most expensive chocolate.

People who enter a business deal
with excess enthusiasm often exit the
deal with excess tears. Healthy skepticism
helps prevent an unhealthy loss.

Intelligent people use the word "impossible" with great caution.

Guys who don't ask girls for dates usually don't have any dates.

Certain large charities enlist the aid of corporate and government officials to help them raise money. These officials then put great pressure on those beneath them to give generously. If a charity must raise money by extortion, then it's not a worthwhile charity at all. Never give your money to those who apply pressure.

Contrary to what our pride might lead us to believe, God is never "on our side." We can of course, if we wish, be on God's side.

Terrorism is the fruit which grows from the seeds of injustice.

You can't be a Methodist and be a Christian, you can't be a Baptist and be a Christian, you can't be a Catholic and be a Christian; but you can be a Christian and be a Methodist, you can be a Christian and be a Baptist, or you can be a Christian and be a Catholic. What we truly are is mainly determined by how we first define ourselves.

Children who are allowed to own toy guns are also usually allowed to point them at people. Children should never be allowed to point toy guns at people!

Our problems usually get bigger when we focus within ourselves. If we wish to see life's rainbows we have to look outward, on the world which surrounds us.

41

The primary importance of most businesses is in the jobs they provide. The world can survive without most products, but it would have a hard time surviving if there were no jobs.

42

There are three types of people: Leaders, followers, and take-chargers. Take-chargers are often considered leaders, but in actuality they are just people whose egos enable them to believe that they should boss everyone else around. Real leaders are usually humble. They are placed in their position by people who demand that they take the lead.

43

Many people are slaves to style, and wouldn't be caught dead in something out of fashion. Thank God for kids who have the guts to wear purple hair.

The more intelligent the person, the less they can be swayed by advertising.

⚜

If people can't be trusted in matters of money, they rarely can be trusted elsewhere.

46

Many important people have
used the advice of psychics to make
major life decisions. Perhaps the most
famous of these people was
Adolf Hitler.

Most deaths in airplane crashes are caused by fire. This being the case, perhaps we should wear fire-retardant clothing when flying.

47

It's usually a mistake to
start a war before raising an army
to march behind you.

48

The smaller the mind,
the greater its ability to ridicule.

Possessing great knowledge
can be extremely useful, but it can never
guarantee happiness or success.
These things depend mainly on
how we use our knowledge, not on
how much of it we've got.

Those who toot their own horn
never make the sweetest music.

⟨~~⟩

Too often we get impatient
with older drivers. It is well to remember
that someday we may
be older drivers too.

Many doctors refuse to give patients copies of their own health records! If a doctor isn't willing to trust you with your own records, then you can assume that the doctor shouldn't be trusted with your health care.

The best husbands
regularly send love notes and
little gifts to their wives.
Wives usually like that!

52

⚬━━⚬

Having money does not always
make one wealthy, nor does the lack
always make one poor.

When the nation is in great danger, the government encourages people to pray. When the prayers are answered, and the crisis is over, the government then tries to keep people from praying.

53

Swinging on grapevines can
be great fun – except for their nasty
habit of breaking!

Terrorism can never be
controlled by restricting freedom.
It can only be controlled by
restricting hate.

Dolls with cloth faces and silly smiles always have better personalities than dolls with plastic heads and perfect smiles.

In times past, slaves did not gladly submit to chains. Today, many do. They gladly put on the chains of the welfare state – and these can be the hardest to break.

Most "couch potatoes" complain that rock climbing is crazy. Many rock climbers say that extreme skiing is crazy. About everybody thinks that road luge is crazy. So long as people aren't endangering others, we probably shouldn't malign the things that they do.

You must have training and
a license to drive a car, but neither
to have a kid. Raising a child is the
greatest responsibility one can
have – most people take
it too lightly.

58

Neglecting to properly care for dogs and cats is often rewarded with fines or imprisonment. Forcing injured horses to run hard and win races is often rewarded with honor and riches.

We often get too hyper over racial matters! Humans will always find reasons to divide themselves, and if we aren't hating each other because of race, we'll do it because of social status or politics or religious affiliation. If racial harmony cured all ills, the world would never have had naked natives running around eating one another. Divisions aren't caused by the color of our skin, but by the condition of our souls.

60

How well we treat the things that we borrow is a good indicator of how much we respect those we borrow from.

If everybody made illegal copies of the things they like to read or hear or watch, writers and performers would starve to death. The human race might then die of boredom!

Very few people
take time to smell flowers.

Marvelous adventures are
often found just beyond our doorsteps.
Unfortunately, few people have any
desire to step out and find them.

Intelligent people always give more respect to those who feed and protect them than to those who merely entertain them.

64

❦

The more we talk about our aches and pains, the less others seem interested in listening.

In general, the people who have the most money live in modest houses and drive ordinary cars. Those who flaunt their money seldom have much of it.

Contrary to popular opinion, most women would not like to live in castles. This is probably just as well; most men couldn't afford one.

66

Toys are good for children;
they are also good for adults. Adults
should always have toys!

Pets that live in the house
tend to have worse personalities than pets
that live outside of the house.

In reality, there's not always much to celebrate about getting married. Anybody can get married, and most everyone does – sometimes more than once. What's really worth celebrating is a union of love – in a marriage which has lasted a lifetime.

68

When exploring tight cave passages, the largest person should always go in first, and always come out last. This lowers the risk of everyone getting trapped!

We bestow honor and wealth
on those who perform our favorite music,
but we seldom give thought to who
created the music. The world is full of
people who can perform a song well,
but there is only one who could
have composed it.

Ten million years from now we
probably won't remember the biggest
problem we're having today.

People who refuse to examine
all sides of an issue can never come to
know the whole truth of the issue.

Poverty has an odor, unlike any other, and it can be found in homes across our land. Irrespective of how much a house may be worth, if the stench of poverty is in it, you can be sure that some poor people live there.

It is no more moral to use the police to protect you than it is to protect yourself. The morality of acts does not change simply because they are committed by proxy.

It's almost impossible to be the best, in a given sport or occupation, without having a highly inflated ego.
God hates an inflated ego!

Dead trees frequently
take vengeance on those who try
to push them down.

Women have an extraordinary
ability to overlook the faults in their men.

People who are
adamantly opposed to hunting
never seem adamantly opposed to cars.
Cars, however, kill far more
animals than hunters.

People who weren't there for their children, when the children were young, are almost guaranteed to find that their children won't be there for them, when they get old. For the most part in life, we get back what we give.

In a democracy,
a law does not really exist if the
majority of citizens refuse to obey it.

78

A stable mind can think
deeply about anything. Unstable minds
are too afraid to do so.

We find it moral and acceptable to send our armies to foreign lands and kill those we perceive might be a danger to us. We find it immoral and unacceptable, however, to kill the drug dealers and child molesters who are a danger to us.

79

A laser pointer is one of the
greatest things for entertaining dogs, cats,
and little children – and one of the worst
for entertaining women.

Intelligent people
ask lots of questions. The rest have too
much pride to ask.

If a stockbroker tries to convince you to put your money in an investment, first find out how well the broker manages his own money. If he hasn't made a fortune for himself, then he probably can't make one for you either.

Violence in movies begets violence in society. Promiscuity in movies begets both promiscuity and violence.

Those who do damage to
the environment almost always see
virtue in the things that they do.

People's intelligence can never
be determined from the size of their
bank accounts.

Churches that spend more
on carpet, than they spend feeding the
hungry, aren't really churches at
all – just glorified social clubs.

To simply talk with someone lonely
is often the greatest gift that we can give.

Music is often a picture of the mind of its creator. The music we prefer often paints a picture of what we truly are within. Beauty tends to beget beauty. Disharmony tends to beget disharmony.

Our society needs to prioritize:
Incredible amounts of time and money
are spent trying to regulate our use of
vitamins, guns, and toys considered
hazardous. If we really cared about
human carnage, we'd do whatever it
takes to get drunks off the highways.
The Bible says something about
"strain at a gnat and swallow a camel."

86

What is done out of hate,
anger, or fear is usually wrong. What is
done out of love is usually right.

Countless trees gave
their lives so that we might read.

Good leaders are
always good listeners.

Bold people are usually
successful; cowards usually are not.
Analyzing things to death
can also insure failure.

Spouses who have a hard time saying "I'm sorry" also have a hard time saying "I love you." Marriages would last a lot longer if these words were spoken more often.

Most anyone can make big money.
What takes brains is doing it so that
others are not hurt.

90

The movement to unite all churches is a foolish and dangerous one. Having many denominations protects the freedom to worship as one wishes. The world once had essentially one church, and the result was corruption and horror. If we are wise we will never repeat the mistakes of the past.

91

Politicians who are driven around in limousines seem to have forgotten that they are merely public servants. Servants should never be allowed to have better cars than their masters.

92

No matter how knowledgeable
or spiritual a person may be, there is no
substitute for the wisdom that
comes with age.

93

❧

Very few experts
are very expert at what they do.

The healthiest people usually
work hard to maintain their good health.
Few things in this life come free.

94

It is amazing how highly we value
our own opinions – and how foolish our
opinions often turn out to be.

People who were exceptionally good looking, when they were young, often grow up to be quite ordinary looking. Children who are not so attractive often turn out to be the best looking adults. For the most part, "every dog [has] his day."

A good wreck, once in a while, breaks the monotony of life.

The more we imitate the traditions of primitive societies, the more we will become like primitive societies.

Several people can look at a pencil and each will see it somewhat differently. Because each of our minds is different, it is impossible to see a given object or situation exactly as someone else would see it. If we are to live at peace with one another, we must be willing to see things from others' point of view.

You can often judge a company
by the graffiti on its restroom walls.
Where the management is fair and
honest, the graffiti is usually benign.
Where the management treats its people
like dirt, the graffiti is filled with hate.
Never go to work for a company without
first checking the restrooms.

People who have the guts
to rob you with a gun are worthy of
far more respect than those who rob you
with their lawyers and a court of law.

The most awesome and fearful words ever uttered on this planet was when Jesus said "inasmuch as you have done it unto one of the least of these my brethren, you have done it unto me."

100

When fun becomes too much work, it's just not fun anymore.

Our perception of beauty changes with time and understanding. As we come to appreciate the inner beauty in people, their outer beauty gets better too.

The magnitude of our problems is often related to the magnitude of our bad attitudes.

102

P eople who judge others – by the clothes that they wear – are easily fooled.

Every breath we breathe out pollutes the air for others. Every breath others breathe out pollutes the air for us. We should therefore strive harder to do good things in life, thus helping to remedy the damage we do.

103

The current fad of glorifying cultural heritage is mostly folly, and mainly helps to further divide us. None of us should take pride in our ancestry because even the best of our lineages is full of violence and degradation and death. The only thing which exists is the present, and the best we can do is to make the most of it. Our futures are determined mainly by what we do right now – not what our ancestors did before us.

104

The greater our level of inner peace,
the less we need to have music turned on.

In an emergency, most knives
can be sharpened on the frosted edge of
a car door window.

Poverty characterized by ingratitude and obesity should seldom be the object of charity. One of the cruelest and most dangerous things society can do is to help those who are unwilling to help themselves.

106

Zoning laws often ban signs and billboards on the grounds that they distract drivers and cause accidents. Girls in short skirts are far more distracting than billboards, but for some reason zoning lawyers never suggest banning skimpy clothing.

If doctors would prescribe vigorous exercise, instead of tranquilizers, their patients might be healthier, wealthier, and a whole lot calmer.

Hate and love are not emotions, for they do not originate in the chemistry of the brain. Their genesis is much deeper – they emanate from the depths of one's soul.

109

People who chew their fingernails have a bad habit. People who chew their toenails have good flexibility.

110

We don't spend enough time watching sunsets. The world would be a better place if we did.

Intelligent people never ridicule the collection of knowledge. Pieces of knowledge are simply tools, and the more of them we have, the easier it is to find our way thru this life.

111

If the salesperson in a store is extremely good looking, and of the opposite sex, you stand a good chance of spending a lot more money than you intended.

The greatest people
are always humble people.

A stereo microscope is one
of the more useful tools you can own.

People who put graffiti on the property of others are seldom seen putting it on their own property.

114

Those blest with the greatest abilities often put them to the least use.

The most unjust thing in the universe would be for the Hitlers of this world to escape eternal punishment and simply slip into nonexistence when they die, or perhaps have lifetime after lifetime to get things right. Never serve any god who doesn't have a Hell.

116

Many men are extremely good at telling women what they want to hear. Many women are extremely good at believing them.

Gambling is one of the
fastest ways to make the rich richer
and the poor poorer. Once the poor have
lost what little they had, they always rise
up in rebellion – and they always
do it with violence.

If you're too busy to pray, you're too busy.

❦

Marriages would be a lot happier and last a lot longer if spouses would simply hold and caress each other a lot longer.

Anyone who can accurately predict the future could easily make billions in the stock market. Evidently, no one can predict the future!

Children who have few toys
seem to appreciate them more than
children who have lots of toys.

120

❦

If people are not made to fear
doing evil, then they usually will do evil.

People who are vexed by the minor eccentricities of others are rarely happy people. Part of happiness is not magnifying the imperfections around us.

121

The best way to deal with unwanted phone solicitation is to say "no thanks" and then simply hang up. The longer you talk, the greater the chance that you will eventually buy something.

In countries prone to great famine, those who are starving are never fat. This is proof that people can't be overweight if they don't eat. Instead of wasting money on diet fads, we would be better off simply eating less and using our fad money to feed those who are hungry.

123

When making money becomes the most fulfilling thing in one's life, then it usually becomes easy to make money.

Parents often live out their dreams and frustrations thru their children's sports activities. Children, and their sports activities, would be vastly better off if parents would run their mouths less and applaud their kids more.

People who demand that hunters stop hunting animals rarely demand that fishermen stop catching fish. Fish do not appreciate such discrimination!

126

The practice of tipping in restaurants is not always good or fair because the size of the tip is often determined by how good a waitress looks, rather than how well she works.

Politicians who send their citizens to war are rarely willing to go to the battlefield to help their citizens fight.

Wallets are almost never
lost when carried in a front pocket.

Nations never fall because of their
short-term mistakes. They only fall
because of their long-term sin.

It's not always a shame to be poor,
but it's nothing to brag about either.

High heels on shoes can lead to
accidents and health problems. If God
had wanted us on high heels, we would
have all been born with tall heel bones.

Politicians find it easy to
make laws, but difficult to repeal them.
Creating good laws is important, but
it is far more important to get rid
of the unjust ones.

Today we agonize about the dangers of allowing citizens to own guns. When our Founders drafted the Second Amendment to the Constitution, the guns that citizens carried were the same – and just as powerful – as the ones carried by the military. Back then, citizens could be trusted with such responsibility. Good citizens still can!

The most beautiful thing
in all of God's creation – which man
can comprehend – is woman.

The best moments of a vacation
usually occur when you get off the
beaten path and go adventuring where
others seldom go.

People who put their own interests before the interests of others often show up late. People who put others' interests before their own are usually on time. How punctual we are is greatly determined by how much we care about the people around us.

134

With all that we know, and all that we can do, it's easy to believe that this generation is the smartest in human history. Thousands of years ago however, without the aid of computers, great temples and pyramids were engineered, and the circumference of the earth was calculated. How many of us today can do these things? Sir Isaac Newton said it best: "If I have seen further than [others] it is by standing upon the shoulders of Giants."

More often than not, when excessive sums are spent on education, the less educated the kids will be. Desire for learning depends mainly on good parents and good teachers. Money wasted on opulent buildings and bureaucracies mostly lowers the quality of education.

136

Some people care more about
their pets than they care about people.
They forget, however, that when times
get tough, pets can't provide medical
care, or financial help, or even offer a
simple prayer. Pets can love us, but
not like people can love us – if
we allow them to love us.

In reality, it is of little importance that we know the age of the universe. What is important is that we know its Maker.

138

There is too much negativity directed towards people with money. A few people do abuse the power that comes with money, but in the larger picture it's the rich who build factories and houses, and create jobs for the rest of us. If ordinary folks ran the show, we'd probably wind up starving to death.

Few people possess much ability
to learn from the mistakes of others.
Some of us can't even learn from
our own mistakes.

We humans often seem devoid of logic. Alcohol and marijuana are both addictive drugs, yet we reward those who sell the one and imprison those who sell the other.

141

With time, most people do change for the better. We must be willing to embrace their changes if we are to change for the better too.

Patriotism is not a virtue unless
the object of one's patriotism is virtuous.

143

That which is true cannot always
be proven. That which is "proven" is
not always true.

God prefers that we talk to Him more than we talk about Him.

144

The more we welcome criticism of our work, the better our work can become.

Adultery and child molestation have at least one thing in common: They usually do great harm to our kids.

We often judge historical characters by the historical accounts written about them. Historical accounts are often wrong!

146

It is always easier to find something if you believe that it exists. Success is very difficult when there is no faith.

Everything we think, everything we say, and everything we do affects tomorrow – and all the tomorrows after that.

148

The punishment for violating the Law of Gravity can be harsh and cruel. For some reason, however, no one demands that this law be repealed.

The more we find fault in others,
the greater our own faults usually become.

⌐∞⌐

Adults who roller skate seem happier
than adults who don't roller skate – except
maybe for those who just took a hard fall.

Honest people try to pay their bills on time – thieves always try not to.

Parents get great satisfaction
out of watching their children enjoy
the things they created for them.
God gets great satisfaction from
watching us enjoy the
things He created.

151

Intelligence is one thing and one thing only: It is the measure of one's desire to know Truth.

continued from page 1

us to truly think at all, and two plus two seem never to add up to four.

This book is a collection of my observations of people, and situations, and all manner of things. Its purpose is to help the reader see the world thru other eyes and from a different point of view, and perhaps reach conclusions not otherwise possible. It is only when we are willing to see thru the eyes of others that we have a chance of tearing down the walls between us. It is only when we are willing to see, from another's point of view, that we can truly begin to see inside ourselves. My observations aren't perfect because I am not perfect, but hopefully they will convey a view of the world which you may not have had the opportunity to see. As you view my world more clearly, perhaps you can see your world more clearly too.

Other books by Tom Martin:

KENTUCKY ICE
A WINTER ADVENTURE

ISBN 0-930871-02-2, 80 pages, hard cover

This book is a photo documentary of extraordinary phenomenon which few people have been privileged to see – phenomenon which may never be seen again. It pictures towers of ice, over one hundred feet high, standing alone in the forest like silent gendarmes; snow, rolled by the wind into giant doughnuts; delicate needles of ice, taller than a man, growing from the floors of caves; and waterfalls frozen solid. With the aid of forty large color pictures, this book describes how such beautiful creations came to exist, and tells about the unique places where they were found.

These photos are black and white miniatures of the color pictures in **KENTUCKY ICE.**

Other books by Tom Martin:

RAPPELLING

ISBN 0-930871-03-0, 304 pages, 400+ pictures, hard cover

This book is the world's first and only "encyclopedia" of rappelling. Written for the purpose of saving lives, it does so by providing knowledge about the many things which can injure or kill rappellers. Designed for use by beginners and experts, its fourteen chapters provide a huge amount of information about ropes, harnesses, rappel methods, and safety. Forty five different descenders are shown, and their use described in detail. There is also a section on ascending methods and equipment, an extensive index and glossary, and a list of manufacturers of rappel equipment. Most everything of practical importance about the subject of rappelling can be found between the covers of this important text.

These photos are miniatures of the 400+ pictures found in **RAPPELLING.**

WRITE YOUR OBSERVATIONS *HERE*